Living with a Volcano

T0354111

Rob Waring, *Series Editor*

HEINLE
CENGAGE Learning™

Australia • Brazil • Japan • Korea • Mexico • Singapore • Spain • United Kingdom • United States

Words to Know

This story is set in Italy on the island of Sicily [sɪsəli]. It happens near the city of Catania [kətɑːnjə], around a volcano called Mount Etna [etnə].

A **A Volcano.** Read the paragraph. Then label the picture with the correct form of the underlined words.

A volcano is a mountain with a large hole at the top which is called a crater. A large volcano may have hundreds of smaller craters, or cones, on its sides. In an eruption, volcanoes produce very hot, melted rock. When it is under the ground, this hot, melted rock is called magma. Once it comes out of the volcano, the hot rock is called lava. Lava, smoke, and gas come out of a volcano during an eruption. This makes the area around a volcano a dangerous place!

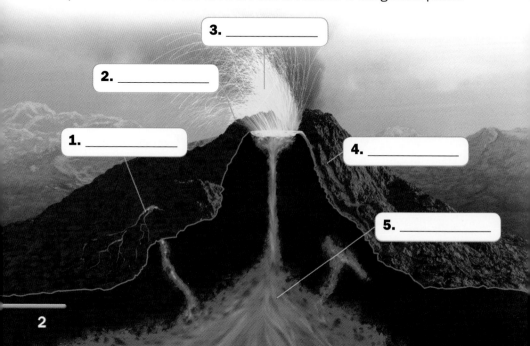

3. _____

2. _____

1. _____

4. _____

5. _____

B Studying Volcanoes. Read the definitions. Then complete the paragraph with the correct form of the words.

> **crust:** another term for the earth's surface
> **unpredictable:** often changing; impossible to guess
> **volcanic ash:** very fine rock that comes out of a volcano during an eruption
> **volcanologist:** a scientist who studies volcanoes
> **tectonic plate:** one of the many large, moving pieces under the earth's surface

Scientists known as (1)_____ study a number of different features of volcanoes. They study the movement of (2)_____ deep under the earth. They also study how these movements formed volcanic openings in the earth's (3)_____ long ago. When a volcano erupts, these scientists examine the lava and (4)_____ that come out of it. They want to know why volcanoes erupt so that they can protect people who live near them. It's difficult to know what these (5)_____ creations will do next!

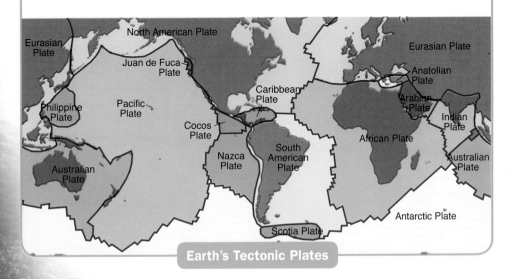

Earth's Tectonic Plates

When Sicily's Mount Etna erupts, it really is a beautiful sight. It looks like an amazing, powerful **fireworks**[1] display and it's the kind of show that everyone notices. However, there's one audience that's watching the volcano for a different reason. It's a small group of scientists who have made watching Mount Etna their life's work. They're volcanologists, and their job is to be on Mount Etna and to watch it very closely.

---

[1]**fireworks:** small objects that produce loud noises and bright colors

Skim for Gist

Read through the entire book quickly to answer the questions.

1. What is the reader basically about?

2. Why is Salvatore Caffo important to the story?

Salvatore Caffo[2] is the main volcanologist on Mount Etna. From his office at Mount Etna National Park, Caffo has an excellent view of the power of the volcano. It's the best place for him to do his job. Caffo's responsibility is to watch the unpredictable mountain and keep records of its activity.

Mount Etna, or simply 'Etna', is more than **10,000 feet**[3] high, which makes it Europe's highest active volcano. The loud noises, smoke and gas that come from the mountain remind everyone that Etna is active. It could erupt at any time.

---

[2]**Salvatore Caffo:** [sælvətɔːri kæfoʊ]
[3]**10,000 feet:** 3,048 metres

Caffo grew up in the city of Catania, which is less than 30 **miles**[4] down the mountain from Etna's craters. He was always extremely interested in the mountain, even as a young boy. He says that when he was just 11 years old, he knew that he wanted to make volcanoes an important part of his life.

At Mount Etna National Park, Caffo's task is important. He must work towards understanding the volcano's role on planet Earth. He must also help others to understand it. Why is this so important? Because, on Etna, there's a very close relationship between man and volcano. There are many people who live on and around this active volcano, so it's very important to always know what's happening. In Caffo's words; 'Mount Etna is a mountain where there's a very strong **interaction**[5] between man and nature. You can't **leave that out of the equation.**'[6]

---

[4] **mile:** 1.61 kilometres
[5] **interaction:** two or more things coming together and affecting each other
[6] **leave (something) out of the equation:** fail to consider an issue when making a decision or planning

Infer Meaning

1. Who is Caffo referring to when he uses the word 'man'?

2. According to Caffo, what fact about Etna must be remembered?

Man and nature have lived together on Mount Etna for centuries, but the volcano has been around for far longer. Mount Etna began to form 600,000 years ago. It began at the place where the African and Eurasian tectonic plates come together, deep under the surface of the earth. On Etna, there are more than 100 craters and cones in a huge volcanic area. These craters and cones indicate the places where gases and magma escape from under the earth's crust.

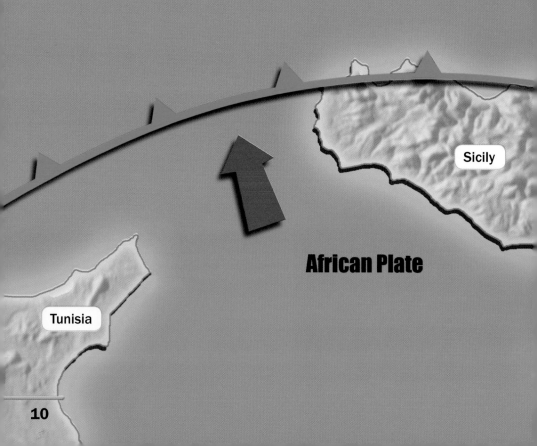

Sicily

African Plate

Tunisia

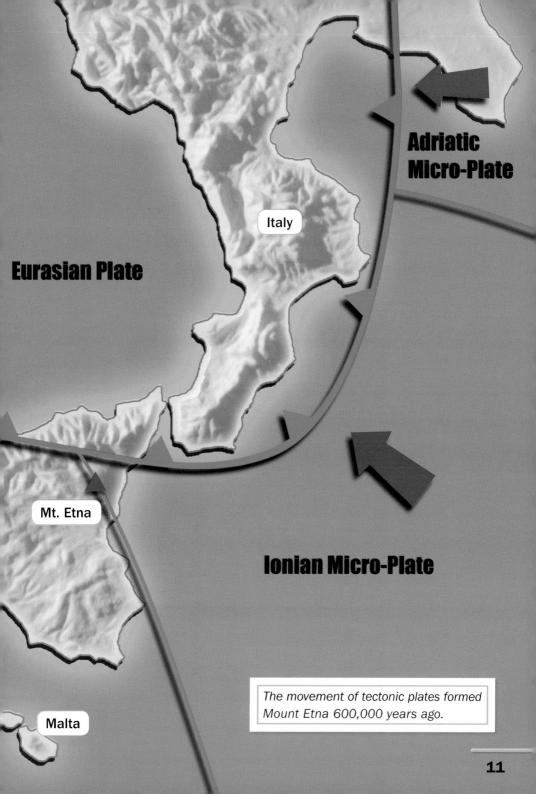

Adriatic
Micro-Plate

Italy

Eurasian Plate

Mt. Etna

Ionian Micro-Plate

Malta

The movement of tectonic plates formed
Mount Etna 600,000 years ago.

Today, thousands of people live on and around the volcano. The volcanic ash makes excellent farmland. For centuries, people have been farming the rich volcanic earth and growing their food near the volcano. Now, many people are also making money from tourists who come to see the eruptions.

Although people have been living on Etna for a long time, it doesn't mean that it's an easy place to live. The town of Nicolosi is just 12 miles down the hill from the crater. The village was first built more than 800 years ago, but eruptions from Etna have destroyed it twice. The people who live in the village know that Nicolosi could be destroyed by Etna again. Yet, the town also benefits from being so close to the volcano. It's an interesting relationship between man and land. The **mayor**[7] of Nicolosi explains: 'There is the risk. We know that. We are **conscious of**[8] this risk. If it's destroyed, well, we rebuild.'

---

[7]**mayor:** leader of a town or city usually chosen by the people of the town
[8]**(be) conscious of:** know about; be aware of

Nicolosi is not the only town in the area that the volcano has affected. There are over 20 small towns which lie around the bottom of the volcano. **Zafferana Etnea**[9] is one of them. It is eight miles from Nicolosi and on the southeastern side of Mount Etna. It's another town that knows the dangers of the volcano very well.

In 1991, an eruption started on Etna which lasted more than 400 days. It covered a whole **valley**[10] that is near Zafferana Etnea with lava. The woods, fields, animals and water were all covered by a red-hot flow of lava. When the people of Zafferana Etnea saw the lava, they were terrified that it was going to reach their town and destroy it.

---

[9] **Zafferana Etnea:** [dzɑːfərɑːnə ɛtneɪə]
[10] **valley:** area of low land between hills or mountains

In 1991, a 400 day eruption of Etna nearly covered an entire valley.

In the end, the lava flow stopped just a few hundred metres from the town. Now, there is a **religious statue**[11] at the place where the lava stopped. People go there to give thanks that the town was saved.

Living so close to Mount Etna has caused people in the area to accept the danger. They know that the volcano will erupt again. It can't be avoided. They just don't know when it will happen – maybe today, maybe tomorrow. One man who lives in Zafferana Etnea feels that in 1991, it was their turn to be in danger. But, he adds, the next time it may be another town. 'That time it was us. This time it's them', he says. 'Maybe in ten years it will be Linguaglossa's turn, or Randazzo's – it's like that. You get used to it. You live with it, and so it doesn't **scare**[12] you.'

---

[11] **religious statue:** a figure which represents a culture's beliefs in a god or gods
[12] **scare:** make frightened; terrify

The people who live around Etna understand the volcano because they are so close to it. They realise that the volcano plays an important role in life on Earth. In fact, according to Caffo, volcanoes are an important part of the world's environmental system. If there were no Etna, life on Earth would be very different. 'I hope that people understand the big importance of this **thermodynamic**[13] machine', he says. 'Without [the] volcano, there isn't ... life.'

---

[13]**thermodynamic:** connected to the relationship between heat and other types of energy

For some, the volcano plays another important role; this time it's a social one. It can help people to understand their own place, or their role in life on Earth. Caffo spends much of his time walking around the volcano. He often explores the black land that is covered with dried lava and examines the ancient craters. For him, Etna influences his approach to life in general. It reminds him of the fact that he is very small when he compares himself with the size of the earth!

Mount Etna is always changing, so it is very interesting for volcanologists. The Pian del Lago cone, for example, is Etna's newest feature. It erupted for the first time in July 2001. When it erupted, it was truly amazing. The pressure was so powerful that lava shot a quarter of a mile into the air! Huge black clouds of smoke and ash erupted out of the crater, as gases from deep within the earth were released.

100 metres

In 2001, Mount Etna erupted and lava shot about a quarter of a mile into the air!

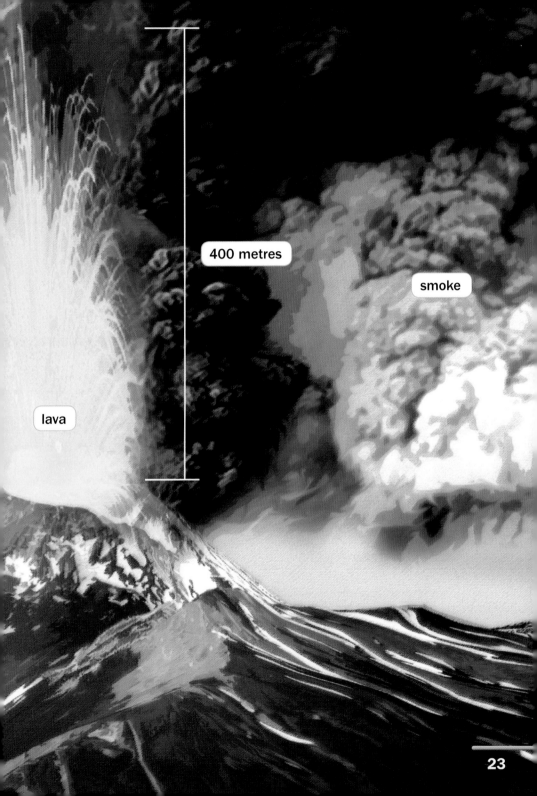

400 metres

smoke

lava

On Etna, there is always something new for Caffo to study. He works with mountain guides and other scientists to survey Etna's eruptions. He tests the lava, measures gases, and looks for surface changes. These elements can provide signs of what is happening under the earth.

Etna has technically been active since 1995, and any eruption is still very exciting for volcanologists. 'When you smell the **sulphur**[14] in the air, it gives you **shivers down your spine**![15] This is the birth, the creation of new earth', explains Caffo.

---

[14]**sulphur:** a yellow chemical element that has an unpleasant smell
[15]**shivers down (one's) spine:** feelings of emotion so strong that they become physical

Sequence the Events

What is the correct order of the events? Write numbers.

_____ The town of Nicolosi was built.

_____ The Pian del Lago cone erupted.

_____ Mount Etna first formed.

_____ There was an eruption that lasted more than 400 days.

Caffo explains that it's not easy to know what the volcano will do next. Even with all of their studies, scientists still don't always understand what's happening deep within the earth. Mount Etna remains as unpredictable as it has always been. For Caffo and the other scientists who study it, that's part of their interest. If they always knew Etna's next move, their job wouldn't be very challenging. In the end, it's Mount Etna's surprises that make Caffo's job exciting. Nobody knows what Etna will do next!

After You Read

1. When does the small group of scientists watch Mount Etna?
   A. in the morning
   B. annually
   C. twice a week
   D. all the time

2. Smoke from Mount Etna shows that it is an active volcano.
   A. True
   B. False

3. What view is expressed by Salvatore Caffo on page 8?
   A. People should not live near Etna.
   B. Man and the nature are linked.
   C. People forget about the volcano.
   D. Nature is stronger than man.

4. Match the cause to the effect.
   Effect: A volcano is formed.
   A. Magma flows down.
   B. A crater erupts.
   C. Tectonic plates come together.
   D. Gases come out from the earth.

5. For the people in Nicolosi, living near Etna has both _____
   and _____.
   A. benefits, risks
   B. farmland, mountains
   C. benefits, good points
   D. mountains, hills

6. How many small towns are near Mount Etna?
   A. two
   B. eight
   C. twenty
   D. four hundred

7. Which of the following is a good heading for page 16?
   A. Which Town Is Next?
   B. Randazzo Saved
   C. Eruption Happens Again
   D. People Are Scared

8. On page 19, Caffo calls Etna a 'machine' because the volcano:
   A. is not natural
   B. has a job
   C. destroys the environment
   D. is near people

9. What's the main point on page 20?
   A. to describe the volcano in detail
   B. to present Caffo's emotions
   C. to talk about peoples' size
   D. to show the volcano's effect on people

10. What happened when the Pian del Lago cone erupted?
   A. Ash shot a mile into the air.
   B. Etna's oldest feature was made.
   C. Lava exploded from the crater.
   D. Red smoke went high in the sky.

11. In the second paragraph on page 24, 'this' refers to:
   A. an eruption
   B. sulphur
   C. an active volcano
   D. a scientist

12. Scientists consider Etna's actions to be:
   A. logical
   B. challenging
   C. simple
   D. predictable

Volcanoes
ON THE MOON

Researchers are very knowledgeable about the nature of the Moon. They have taken detailed photographs and space travellers have brought rocks back from the Moon's surface. By studying these, scientists have discovered that the Moon has had many volcanic eruptions in the past. They have also found that volcanoes on the Moon are very different from those on Earth.

Age and Position of Volcanoes on Earth and the Moon

The Moon and Earth both have volcanoes.

Although both sites have experienced significant volcanic activity, there are clear differences between them. There are still many active volcanoes on Earth that could erupt at any time. Most of the volcanoes on Earth are about 100,000 years old. However, the Moon's volcanoes are between three and four billion years old and are no longer active. A second major difference is their position. Volcanoes on Earth are fairly evenly distributed around the tectonic plates. Most of the Moon's volcanoes are on only one side.

Volcanoes on the Moon are low and broad.

The Influence of Tectonic Plate Activity

Volcanologists look carefully at tectonic plate activity. On Earth, volcanic activity usually happens very close to mountains. This is where the movement of tectonic plates is the strongest. On the Moon, however, there doesn't seem to be any tectonic plate activity. Instead, the volcanoes seem to occur wherever the crust of the Moon is thinnest. Scientists have suggested that the crust is thinnest on the side of the Moon that is closest to Earth. This could be one reason why many volcanoes are found there.

Size and Shape of Volcanoes on Earth and the Moon

On Earth, there are many tall volcanoes. Tall volcanoes are formed by strong eruptions with many layers of volcanic ash and lava. This results in a cone-shaped volcano with an empty crater inside. On the Moon, however, the eruptions were gentler. Therefore, the results were quite different – a broad, thin coating of lava over the surface of the Moon. This created the low, wide volcanoes which we find there.

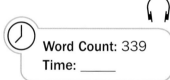
Word Count: 339
Time: _____

Vocabulary List

cone (2, 10, 22, 25)
(be) conscious of (12)
crater (2, 8, 10, 12, 20, 22)
crust (3, 10)
eruption (2, 3, 4, 7, 12, 14, 16, 22, 24, 25)
fireworks (4)
interaction (8)
lava (2, 3, 14, 16, 20, 22, 23, 24)
leave (something) out of the equation (8)
magma (2, 10)
mayor (12)
mile (8, 12, 22)
religious statue (16)
scare (16)
shivers down your spine (24)
sulphur (24)
tectonic plate (3, 10, 11)
thermodynamic (19)
unpredictable (3, 7, 27)
valley (14)
volcanic ash (3, 12)
volcanologist (3, 4, 7, 22, 24)